Saved, Unwed & Motherhood

Valerie P. Laster

WestBow
P R E S S
A DIVISION OF THOMAS NELSON

WestBow Press books may be ordered through booksellers or by contacting:

WestBow Press
A Division of Thomas Nelson
1663 Liberty Drive
Bloomington, IN 47403
www.westbowpress.com
1-(866) 928-1240

Because of the dynamic nature of the Internet, any web addresses or
links contained in this book may have changed since publication and
may no longer be valid. The views expressed in this work are solely those
of the author and do not necessarily reflect the views of the publisher,
and the publisher hereby disclaims any responsibility for them.

Any people depicted in stock imagery provided by Thinkstock are
models, and such images are being used for illustrative purposes only.

Certain stock imagery © Thinkstock.

ISBN: 978-1-4497-6771-6 (sc)
ISBN: 978-1-4497-6770-9 (e)

Library of Congress Control Number: 2012917596

Printed in the United States of America

WestBow Press rev. date: 10/29/2012

CONTENTS

Dedication

To Mrs. Eunice Stephens, my high school English and Journalism instructor: Thank you for all of the inspiration and encouragement. You said I would be an awesome author and thus, I have taken the plunge.

To my son David who has been such an inspiration and has been so positive: Thanks for all of your help with this project and your moral support.

Forever grateful,

Valerie/Mom

Note: I am indeed a believer in Jesus Christ, but in this book I will not overwhelm you with the Bible or scripture although there will be some scriptures quoted and scriptural references. This is plain talk.

This book is dedicated to all women who love the Lord, are unwed, and are mothers or are in the motherly way. My message to you is: "Everything will be and is all right. God still loves you and there is nothing that will ever change that." Do not beat yourself down or feel ashamed because you are a human being and all human beings are fallible.

You are now positioned to make many quality, long-term life changing decisions for yourself, your child and your relationship with the Lord, that is all there is to it. You are still loved and valued.

What is meant when an individual says he or she is "saved"? There is no need to go as far as some people do to explain the terminology. If some folks are asked if they are saved, the answer is and I quote: "I am saved, sanctified, filled with the Holy Ghost on my way to heaven and glad about it"....whew... that is a mouthful, but to each, his own. The true meaning is the person has accepted Christ as his or her Savior and experiences a positive spiritual life change; a spiritual new birth.

To be "saved" does not mean a person will not falter. Everyone falters along their journey – NO ONE IS PERFECT. Misjudgment of situations and people along the way will happen, however, the Lord is there to redeem each and every one of us from and through these situations to make the situation work out in a positive manner. There will be pain, disappointment and some other not-so-good feelings and experiences during this journey, but the Lord's healings and blessings will continue to flow and manifest in the lives of His children. Do not ever let anyone take that from you.

One of the biggest lies I believed for years was that everyone else was walking this journey perfectly well and I was messing up and stumbling all along the way --- wrong. Just because you do not see other peoples' errors or wrongdoings does not mean the mistakes are not there or do not exist. There is a saying: **everyone has skeletons in the closet** ---- **everyone!!!**: the preacher, teacher, pastor, apostle, prophet and lay member.

Although you are an unwed mother, you certainly are not an outcast. The Lord will not and has not thrown you away. You will not suffer an insatiable eternal hell because you are with child and unwed. And guess what…God still loves you and will make provisions for you to care for your child and yourself should you decide to single parent, co-parent, marry, etc. God loves your child too, planned or not, whether you are married or not.

Keep in mind that just because you have a child or children out of wedlock does not mean you will not become a doctor, lawyer, writer, teacher or preacher. You still have talents that are useful and each experience you have will enhance and create many more useful talents within. You will grow as a woman, mother and friend to yourself.

The difficulties we bring upon ourselves and those that are put upon us can and may cause delay(s) of some sort to God's perfect plan for our lives, but God is still in control of your life and destiny, and He will manifest what He needs to manifest in your life when the time is right. If anyone says differently, they are lying absolutely. You do not have to have a perfect slate in order for God to bless you or use you. **There are no perfect people.**

To attend church frequently does not relieve us of the need for or desire to be loved by someone of the opposite sex.

If you are the type of female who physically desires relations with a man, do not let anyone steer you in the other direction. Ask the Lord for a mate. It is perfectly fine to ask the Lord for a mate. The Lord wants each of us to be fulfilled spiritually, mentally, emotionally and physically. Keep in mind some people are more family-oriented than others. If your friend does not want a husband, that is all right for her. If you desire a husband, that is fine as well.

Some people mature more rapidly than others. Your friend may not be ready for marriage or a family until she is 35-years-old, but you may be ready for marriage at 19-years-old. Each person has different needs, desires and destiny. This is why there should never be comparisons amongst people. Many couples marry at an early age, (i.e., 19 or 21-years-old) and live a happily married life for years. Some do not marry until age 40 or 50-years-old and remain happily married. On the other hand, some people marry and the marriage does not last at all. Which is right? You must do what is necessary and good for you. Follow the unfolding of **your** life, not someone else's life.

CHAPTER I

Your Relationship with God

Let me begin by saying that once you receive Jesus into your heart, He will love you and be there for you no matter what the circumstance. Jesus will never leave you. People will turn away and talk about you in a negative manner, but God never, ever will. People will judge you – but only God's judgment will stand. As a matter of fact, God loved you long before you even knew him. So, believe you me, you can depend on the Lord despite any situation you find yourself.

Jesus' love is the primary example of unconditional love towards you. **He** died on the cross for your sins – "For God so loved the world, that he gave his only begotten Son, that whosoever believeth in Him should not perish, but has everlasting life." (King James, John 3:16)

The Lord understands why you are in this situation. There are so many, many reasons why people make the decisions they make and guess what…God's love flows anyway…it will be all right no matter what may transpire. God cares about you and your situation, your future. Yes, you do have a future.

God is not going to leave you behind. He will not turn his back on you. (People might but, He will not). Why not you might ask? Because now is when you need Him the most. Think about that…**now is when you need the Lord the most**.

What type of God or friend would He be if He left you during your most difficult time(s)? Should you decide to carry your child full-term and parent, adopt out or even if you decide to abort, God will continue to love you. Hopefully, you will choose life, but whatever you do, He will **always** love you. There is no end to **always,** nor is there an end to His love for you and your unborn child.

Please, do not mistake what I have stated as a license to sin and destroy others or yourself, but to know that when you make a mistake or two or three or four, He is there to recover you and help you to recover because He does not want to lose you or your child. However, He does want you to make choices that will enhance and strengthen your life.

Did you sin? According to the Bible - Yes. Is sin forgivable? Yes. That is why Jesus came. The Bible says, "…And if any man sin, we have an advocate with the Father, Jesus Christ the Righteous." (King James, I John 2:1): "If we confess our sins, he is faithful and just to forgive us *our* sins, and to cleanse us from all unrighteousness." (King James, I John 1:9). Believe you me, we all have had to embrace these two scriptures throughout our journey, and will continue to do so.

The Healing Process

To begin your healing process, you need to talk to the One that made you --- not man, woman, boy or girl but God. Fall on your knees and pray, seek His face and let Him fix the situation, your life. Let the Lord heal the hurt and the shame. This is the first step to solving any problem.

What does that mean? There are so many possibilities that may come from this one situation. Maybe the Lord will allow you and the gentleman to marry, maybe not. Maybe the Lord will give you the support system you need to be a single parent (not everyone is cut out for single parenting), or maybe He will allow you to place your child with a mom and dad that will love your child without reservation. Whatever the outcome, the Lord is right there with you and your child each and every step of the way.

This decision must be yours and yours alone, because you are the one who will have to live with the decision and its outcome and ramifications. Ask yourself, can I live with the decision to single parent, can I live with the decision to place my child with a loving family, can I live with the decision to marry this man and raise my child.

A huge part of the healing process is emotional. To be accepted by those who love you despite the situation is a huge step towards the emotional healing in this matter. Nothing is more refreshing than to know that the people who were disappointed by the choices you made - love you anyway. These types of situations teach each of us to love others during their times of challenge and struggle.

Love and accept yourself as well as the choices you made, whether those decisions brought about positive or negative effects. There is something to be learned. Never ever throw yourself away, even if or when others do. I have a saying: "I am stuck with me for a lifetime – no matter who comes or goes – it is me with me all the way." Another one is: "No matter who comes and goes, I am struck with me forever, so I trump everyone else – what they say really does not matter." Learn to be YOUR OWN BEST FRIEND.

Being saved, unwed and a mother can encourage you to walk closer to the Lord. Do not give up, continue loving the Lord because he truly loves you and by all means, learn to love yourself unconditionally. This is your journey.

CHAPTER II

In Your Heart of Hearts, What Outcome Do You Desire?

Be honest with yourself. When you are alone, do you desire to be married, single, co-parent, adopt or just not be a mother at all? Let us look at each possibility.

Marriage

Do you love the father of your unborn child enough to marry him? On the other side of that, does he love you enough to nurture you and this little person into adulthood and the three of you function as a healthy family unit? These are key questions to the marriage decision (not the only questions, but key questions).

Many people choose to marry to avoid the shame and embarrassment of becoming an unwed mother and find themselves in an abusive situation. Before you know it, the marriage is over and the woman and child have only a name and a legal battle for child support and custody.

Are you prepared to be a mother and a wife? Well, even if you are not, can you be made ready? Are you open to the preparation process of wifehood and motherhood? If the answer is yes, this situation can bring you and your partner together as a healthy family unit and can offer many rewards. This may be what your potential husband wants and needs, and consequently, this may be what you truly want and need as well. Discuss it with your partner - not with your girlfriend - but with your mate so the two of you can come to the best decisions for the three of you. Give him a chance and keep a mature perspective. You can handle whatever the outcome.

Be mindful that this situation is not the end of your life; your life will go on and progress. There will be many life lessons and choices you will face during your journey and when you look back on your life you want to be able to say <u>you made the best decisions the best way you knew how with the knowledge and insight you possessed at that time</u>.

Seek counseling from someone in loving authority, whether it is your mother and/or father, a trained certified counselor, or someone you respect and love (a teacher, a priest/rabbi/pastor). Lay hold of the solid healthy information you need to make sound decisions from someone who is not going to judge you and put you down but steer you in a healthy direction, someone with whom you can be totally honest.

Note: **Whatever you do, do not marry an abusive man. If your partner is abusive, allow him to get the needed counseling and continue said counseling for at least 2 years before you consider an engagement. He should undergo counseling consistently and work through his abuse issues before you consider a more permanent situation. If he does**

not agree to the counseling and help he needs, do not marry this man because he will only abuse you and your child.

Listen to your heart of hearts and make the decision that is right for you. And above all else, pray and ask the Lord for guidance. It is never too late for Him to step in.

My Testimony

In my early 30's I relocated to Colorado Springs, CO. Shortly thereafter, I began spending time with a Christian gentleman. One thing led to another and I became pregnant.

Once he found out about my pregnancy, early on he determined he did not wish to be a father or husband. I had to respect that and come to terms with his personal decision. With just having left an abusive church relationship and having blindly walked into a relationship with a man who did not want a relationship or a child...immediately my decision was to go through this pregnancy alone, or at least, definitely without him. In my mind, based upon our conversations, he was not husband or father material for me or my son.

Well, people tried to talk me into marrying this man. A man who had been twice married and had mentally and emotionally abused his past wives; and a man who had abandoned me and my child early on. No way was marriage a consideration.

Today my son is 20-years-old and is a responsible young man. What a delight he has been and an inspiration to me. The Lord spoke to me about my son early on. He promised me my son would not be a hardship and would be easy to rear. God was so right. I can honestly say without reservation, my son was a good kid and a pleasure to rear. He was loveable and quite energetic. A little mouthy at times, but when it comes down to it, he was and is a nice guy. Thank you Lord Jesus.

Some people say single parents produce criminals because the father is absent. I totally disagree. Many times if the father is in the household he can be abusive to the children and the woman – that is not God's best for any woman or child and I refused to subject myself or my child to this sickness as should every mother.

Thanks to my Pastor who counseled me and helped me through this really tough time and tough decision. I can truly say the correct decision was made in my situation; there are no regrets on my part.

Single Parenting

Single parenting can work well when the single parent has a strong personal constitution, a strong network of support, a strong work ethic (and by work that means at home as well as in the workplace) and lots of love and patience to give. Not everyone is a good candidate for single parenting. It takes a special type of person to walk this road. You must be a strong, smart, loving, flexible and determined person. You need a support network or team. The support network can come from church, family, extended family via friends or otherwise.

Education can also be a type of support. Education has played an important role in the lives of many single parents. Even our President, President Obama, has encouraged single mothers to go back to school to get an education to better support their children and in order to thrive in this world. What a wonderful gift he is offering the women and children of our nation. Once you are situated and settled into your new role of motherhood, consider taking some college courses and matriculate at the appropriate time. College is an activity that may keep you focused and help set a positive tone for lives of your child(ren) as well.

Keep in mind, becoming a single parent can happen in any number of ways. It can be the result of a divorce, the death of a spouse and/or becoming a single parent by choice or just by everyday circumstances. Whatever the impetus, single parenting is a very important role.

Single parents wear many different hats and play different roles. Sometimes he/she will feel stretched very thin emotionally and physically. Therefore, remember to always reserve time for yourself. Proper exercise, diet and a healthy social life are important to be a continuous healthy influence to your child or children.

Many people abuse their children because they feel stressed beyond normalcy. Extreme stressors along with the issue of non-social activity with other adults in many cases, lead to abuse.

If you feel out of control and as if you may hurt your child, get help immediately. There is no greater embarrassment than the embarrassment of standing before a police officer or judge with regard to how you have mistreated a little person. So, stay socially active and connected and have a life apart from your responsibilities and you will be fine.

If you decide to keep your child, you do not want to keep the child based upon promises that people make to you (i.e., I will help you raise the baby; if you need me, I will be there; etc.). Although, people mean well, none of us knows what the future holds. Those who make the promises may move away, have children of their own, get a job in another state, get sick or even die. This is your decision. Which decision can you live with based upon your belief system? The saying goes "It takes a village to raise a child" but do you trust the village with your child's well being? Hopefully you do not trust the villagers with your children because there are a lot of shady characters in most villages.

My Testimony

Once I decided to single parent, the Lord blessed me beyond measure. After my release from the hospital, there were people in my church who loved me so much and helped me get through that rough time and I will be forever grateful.

One friend came to my house and cleaned; one friend washed my clothes; another friend came over with a blank check from an acquaintance who gave instructions to purchase whatever I needed for my son. Wow. God is in the blessing business.

My friend Karla would come over and walk with me and talk with me to keep depression from taking a stronghold in my life during this time. There were people around me who truly loved the Lord, me and my son and through much prayer and supplication we made it through that tough time.

If I never pray again, I surely prayed during that time. I say thank you to all of the people and friends who loved me and my son and helped me through such a tough time. I truly am grateful and I love you too. Thank you, Lord, for true Christian friends.

I went through counseling with my Pastor and he was thorough and did not pull any punches. He also did not judge me but he loved me. I will never forget him saying to me that God's best is not for us to be abused by anyone and he did not recommend marriage.

It sometimes takes someone else to bring us around to accept the realities of life when we are in tough places. My Pastor looked at the situation as it was and gave his honest Godly counsel and guess what, the people in my church loved on me and my son. So many blessings came upon me because I allowed the Lord to come in and I told the truth and did not hide my situation. The Lord will do the same for you.

Shared Parenting or Co-Parenting

Shared parenting or Co-parenting is where the courts today have been directing couples with regard to the care of children in the midst of divorces and breakups. This way the child still has a mother and father in his/her life. It is good for the child to maintain a sense that both parents still love and care even though each parent may reside in a different residence, city or state.

This parenting style works for many people. Even though each parent has made a different choice with regard to whom he or she will be in a love relationship with, both parents have made the important decision to be in the life of the child and live out their roles. To be honest, the parties involved have to respect and love themselves, the other person and the child for this scenario to work effectively.

The real questions are, can you handle seeing the other parent and not be with him? Can you handle seeing the other parent with someone else whom he has decided to share his life with other than you? Can you interact with this person and work through the resentment, hurt and bitterness without causing a raucous in front of your child? There are many scenarios to consider before going down this road, but it can be fulfilling if both parents put the child first and resolve their differences in a mature manner.

Adoption

Adoption is a viable solution to being a single parent. Find a reputable adoption agency that will counsel you thoroughly and give you the pros and cons of adopting out. Do research and read as much as you possibly can about the subject of adoption. Remember, this may have some negative long-term psychological effects, especially in the realm of guilt. Can you resolve the guilt issues of giving up your child? Did the child actually place with a loving family? Will you consider open or closed adoption? These are just some of the questions you will need to consider.

Let us look at both types of adoption, open and closed. Which avenue do you think will be better for your child, the father and you? Keep in mind that in most states, if the mother does not wish to parent, the father will be approached with regard to parenting without you. This may mean signing over your rights as the mother and the father taking full custody.

Open Adoption: This process allows the birth mother the opportunity to interview and choose the future parents for her child. The birth mother is also allowed to participate in the child's life after giving birth and going through with the adoption process. Please keep in mind, this type of adoption can be healthy or it can keep the birth mother filled with guilt. Each individual should choose what is best for her and the child. The purpose is to make everyone a winner.

Closed Adoption: This adoption process is essentially different in that after the adoption, the birth mother is <u>not</u> involved with the child and in most cases, not allowed to contact the child, know the where-abouts of the child or the residence of the child.

An adoption can be with a relative or a friend of the family as well – it does not have to be with or through an agency. However, an adoption of any type should endure the necessary legal processes to prevent the parents involved from reneging. This does happen and could happen to you, if you do not cover all legal bases.

The decision is yours because you will be the molder and shaper of this young life – be honest with who you are and where you are at this point in your life and try to ascertain your life's direction. If you choose adoption, remember, God still loves you and will love you forever – nothing will ever change that.

Abortion

Abortion is a serious matter and the decision to abort a child should be made with very careful consideration with as much information as you can obtain. Some consider abortion a bad word. If you choose to abort, know that there will be long-lasting consequences. There will be guilt and mental hurt that you are inflicting upon yourself, which residual effects may not be resolvable right away.

Some use abortion as a quick fix and some use abortion as a contraception. This is very unhealthy. If you find yourself having multiple abortions, get some help and get it right away. You are not taking care of yourself if you are aborting pregnancy after pregnancy. You are causing much harm to yourself which may last a lifetime or take a lifetime to undo.

However, if you are in a situation where abortion is the absolute resolve due to illness, rape, incest, etc. still get all the knowledge and information you can prior to making this decision because it is final and cannot be undone. Be honest with yourself and make sure as much as possible this is something you can handle. You will still be loved and God will still be there for you. The choice is yours and you have the right to choose no matter what anyone says.

Is there healing after an abortion? There most certainly is healing afterwards.

If you choose to walk down this road, be careful with whom you share your decision. Not everyone can handle it, especially if they are self-righteous. Self-righteous people will try to put you down and maybe even destroy you.

My Testimony

I became pregnant and absolutely did not want to be a mother again. There was no way I was having another child, it just was not going to happened no way no how. So I decided abortion was the absolute answer for me.

The person I became pregnant with was not someone I wanted in my life at all in that capacity, nor did I want to be a mother again at this time in my life. My mistake was confiding in someone I believed was a true friend. She literally tried to destroy my life.

My point is, no matter what you decide with regard to being an unwed mother, pray and choose wisely those to whom you go for counseling. Some people want to take your rights away and dictate how you should live and the choices you should make. Only you can be accountable for you. If you belong to a church where the leadership does not hold confidentiality in high esteem, do not divulge your real life issues and/or consider finding another church. You do not want to be in a position where leadership uses your personal information against you.

Confidentiality is a necessary trait for a person to possess prior to making them your confidante. Jesus does not tell our business. He does not embarrass us in front of others for their delight. He loves us from the cradle to the grave and He never tells a secret.

If there is lack of confidentiality, there is lack of respect and lack of accountability to others. You want to confide in leaders who are accountable for their actions. Lack of confidentiality from leadership may inflict emotional pain upon the person counseled. *Note:* **There are laws regarding intentional infliction of emotional abuse, so keep this in mind.** And yes, laws apply to the church and church goers as well. Ministers, church faculty and Christians are not exempt from the laws of the land. So, if your confidential counseling sessions are being divulged to the public without your consent – you are being abused, go see a lawyer to determine what your rights are and how to protect them. Yes, you have rights that are protected by the Constitution of the United States and if your rights are being violated, the person or persons violating your rights should be held accountable.

CHAPTER III

Miscellaneous Topics

Is Age a Factor when deciding to keep a child? I want to say – do not let age be a factor in your decision. Many a young girl has turned out to be a good mother and grown into womanhood after bringing forth a child. So, if your maternal instincts are strong and you want to keep your child and are willing to do the work - go for it.

Today young pregnancies are common – there are so many resources available to young single mothers that were not available in the 50's, 60's and 70s, therefore, do not let age deter you from becoming a parent, if this is what you truly want. *(Note:* **This is not a license to live a promiscuous life).** If you are under the age of majority, do not even think about becoming a mother.

I once met a lady who said she was pregnant at the young age of 12. I had never heard of that and did not reply because it was truly out of my train of thought. But, whatever your age, be realistic about your situation when you make your decision because this decision is long-term.

Dating

It is okay to date while single and single parenting? I would say it is absolutely necessary to date and stay connected to social activities and other adults while single parenting. One of the most serious concerns is the type of man you choose to date and when and if to introduce your child(ren) to this person. Also, consider what your motive is for dating. Are you looking for a husband or just a friendly companion?

Dating and Men in the Church

Let us be honest, there are not as many men in the church as there are women. Therefore, many women marry men who are not within the church they attend or not in church period. That is a personal decision. The difference between the two is one carries the name of Christ and the other does not, which is important. If a man does not honor the Lord in the choices he makes, he probably thinks he can do whatever he wants and will not respect women and their feelings. This is a dangerous man because he probably does not care how his actions affect others. Usually men who truly honor God are more compassionate and family-oriented and better suited for marriage.

Men who think just because they are men, all women are to submit to them because women are lesser than they are, are really in a not-so-good place. Real men respect women and recognize their equality through God's eyes - we just play different roles. Many brave and bold women have changed the face of history throughout the ages.

Do not assume for a moment that just because a man is in church he is compassionate. There are abusive men in church. Some pastors and ministers beat their wives and get up and preach in the pulpit. Know the person well before you consider having him meet your child(ren). Investigate to determine if he has a history of dumping women and children. If he does, do not even think about it. If he has a history of long-term relationships and takes good care of his children and respects his ex...date for a while before considering the introduction to your child. You want to make sure, as much as possible, this man is going to be around for the long haul before you consider any type of introduction.

CHAPTER IV

Conclusion

Forgiveness is the key to getting on with your life and living again. Forgive yourself and those who hurt you or made you feel less worthy of self-love and the Love of God. Now this does not come overnight. Anyone who tells you so is less than truthful. Forgiveness is a process. Once the Lord has begun His healing process, then forgiveness will flow.

Forgiveness takes time and all that name-it-and-claim-it crap is just that – crap. You are not a mechanical being, but a human being and when you are hurt you have to deal with the hurt, or in other words - resolve that emotional pain. Once the situation is resolved or begins to be resolved, forgiveness will flow and not until then, so, do not be discouraged if you are unable to forgive right now – it will come in time at the right time.

Reality Check: Those who look down their noses upon you are no better than you are and have committed the same or similar acts in most cases. Most people who are married had sex before marriage, maybe they did not conceive or perhaps they did conceive and got married to hide it. Do not let people fool you or hold you to standards they can not fulfill themselves. Accept yourself for who you are, not for who others want you to be or to become. Your choices make you who you are and help mold who you will become. You have a voice, use it.

Decision

At the end of the day, we all make choices that we believe or hope will enhance and improve our lives. Whatever your choice, God will love you forever and you can believe that. But, you want to make sure that whatever choice you make, that decision will allow you to respect yourself and love yourself once the dust settles.

Our biggest hurdles come from within. We do not have to worry about God's love and forgiveness toward us, we usually have to determine if we can or will forgive ourselves and love ourselves after making certain decisions. Yes you can, and yes you will. You can learn to love and forgive yourself as often as necessary because life is a long journey, some longer than others, but at any rate, it takes a lifetime to understand, know and satisfy God's desire for us, and we do make decisions outside of his perfect will many times during this journey and have to be redirected.

So, whichever choice you make, remember, God is there. He loves you and always will. Be wise.

With Love,

A TOUCH POETRY

FIND A REASON, FIND A WAY

If you can find a reason, you will find a way.

What's your reason? Family, friends, hope for things to come?

Always have a reason to be, to live, to love, to enjoy life, to give.

And oh, how the doors will open and sometimes push you right on through.

Don't give up, don't quit, don't throw in the towel.

Do hold on, do hold out, and in spite of all else – do find a reason.

For, if you can find a reason, you will surely find a way.

Valerie P. Laster

THE SONG OF A BROKEN HEART

How could he do this to me?

He said he loved me so much. We were supposed to be together forever.

How could he leave me and my child and never look back?

How could he not help me at all? We need him doesn't he know…

How could he be happy with someone else? She's not me.

I gave him everything and tried to give more; maybe too much.

How could he have a family with someone else?

I did love you, you know…….

Valerie P. Laster

<u>Senses</u>

Reflections from the past

Widening horizon

Winter in the air

Bright future

Sonorous bells

Humorous laughs

Safe forever

Taking on risks

Freshness of life

Crispness of water

Therefore I am

It's time to move on

David A. Laster

Scripture References:

1. Romans 8:35-39 (love of God)

2. John 3:16 (the love of God)

3. Ephesians 1:5-8 (redemption)

4. Ephesians 2:8 (grace)

5. Romans 8:28 (forgiveness)

6. I Corinthians 13 (love for others and self)

7. II Corinthians 4:8-9 (cast down but not destroyed)

8. Hebrews 12:2-6 (looking unto Jesus)

9. Roman 3:23 (sin)

10. Luke 24:46-47 (Christ/remission of sin)

Printed in the United States
By Bookmasters